REMAIN

REMAIN

Jennifer Murphy

Remain
Poems by Jennifer Murphy
© 2005
All rights reserved
Printed in Canada

Fly by Night Press
A subsidiary of A Gathering of the Tribes, Inc.
P.O. Box 20693
Tompkins Sq. Station
New York, NY 10009
Tel: (212) 674-3778
Fax: (212) 388-9813
E-mail: info@tribes.org
www.tribes.org

Book design and layout: Finley Kipp

Produced by Marquis Book Printing, Inc., a member of Scabrini Group
2700, rue Rachel est
Montreal (Quebec), H2H 1S7
Tel: (514) 954-1131
Fax: (514) 954-0004

ISBN #1-930083-06-8

This publisher is a proud member of

This book was made possible in part with funds from NYSCA

ACKNOWLEDGEMENTS

Versions of some of these poems appeared in the following magazines: *Mississippi Review, Nthposition, A Gathering of the Tribes: Issue 10, Inkwell Magazine, Dead Mule School of Southern Literature, Jack Magazine.* Thank you to those editors.

"Positive" was included in *Bum Rush the Page: A Def Poetry Jam* (ed. Tony Medina), 2001.

"Canvas" was included in *Tattoo Nation* (ed. Chris McAlister), 2005.

Special thanks to Steve Cannon, professor, encourager, publisher, and to my editor, Robert Strong. Thanks to Ellen Bass, Richard Silberg and Lois Griffith for their responses to this collection and help with this manuscript, and to Finley Kipp for her graphic design expertise. Thanks to all those living poets who have greatly influenced my work: Dean Young, Tony Hoagland, Frank Bidart, Mary Oliver.

My endless gratitude to all of those at Tribes and the Nuyorican Poets Café who supported the writing of these poems over the years. Heartfelt thanks to all my friends and loved and deeply loved ones, without whom the completion of this book would have been impossible: Felice Belle, Nancy Park, Sarah John Manges, Paul Abruzzo, Dan Witz, Matt Atkinson, Ned Leavitt, Lynn Margileth, Bridget Turner, Franklin Simonetti, Eben Burr, Affonso Goncalves, Gemma Rothko, Sonya Lea Ralph, Grace Peterson and Brendan Kertin.

Cover Art: Dan Witz, *Untitled*, Brooklyn, NY, 2002.

for my mother,
in loving memory of Hugh and Fern

CONTENTS

I. THE OLD HOUSE

II. LIP

III. FLAME

No one can confidently say that he will still be living tomorrow.
—Euripides

Are you sure you want to Shut Down?
—Microsoft Windows

1. THE OLD HOUSE

. . . I would rather not go
back to the old house . . .

GETTING OVER

Twelve and a half years to get over
leaving a twenty-five year marriage;
five years to forget the endless summers
your daughter drowned in Boone's Farm
in a dirt field at midnight; two years
of chicken noodle soup to heal
the collapsed heart her idiot boyfriend
ruptured, kissing a towheaded cross-
country runner; one month of cigarette
smoke to recall why you quit at thirty,
when you delivered your first son;
ten minutes to come up with his name,
twenty-one when his first suicide attempt
failed, when your age became a stake
in the broken dirt of regret,
marking time spent in the roadside
city of your home where there is no *over*
only *through*, splintered wood to mark
your presence in the desert; fifty-seven
when your daughter's doctor said *malignant*;
seven years for your antique father
to forget your name and die of pneumonic
complications from Alzheimer's disease;
one lifetime to walk three feet
from the deck to the shed, to his ashes
hidden by your second husband
attempting to shield you from further
grief, hard at work in the garage,
building you a new kitchen, hammering
nails into the dead evening as stars

tear through the tarp of sky stretched
so thin across the night you are
surprised it doesn't break and fall
over the wild fern, the silver elm
you planted in '97 when you decided
to love again and meanwhile, sunset—
another twelve hours until dawn.

CAMANCHE ROAD

At some point my parents
acquired a condominium at the beach,

in a sunless, seaside town called Carpinteria,
an hour's drive over the Grapevine

to Highway 101. My father made me
go with them every weekend while my brother,

being five years older and already employed
as a line cook at Bob's Big Boy,

got out of these *quiet*, weekend trips—
something for which I blamed and envied him for

not wanting to go myself. I wanted to stay
home and drink in the soft dirt fields behind Camanche

Road, out past Mesa Merin Raceway and Rio Bravo
Country Club, nothing but dust and tumble

weed, a hundred teenagers chugging Bud Light
out of red plastic cups, kegs stacked in the back

of so many pickup trucks, headlights beaming
through the dark bare fields until we were tottering

and goalless, nothing for miles except lights
from the oil rigs gleaming at the foot of the bluffs,

neon orange glow of cigarette butts radiating
like electrocuted fireflies until the sheriff's department

arrived in helicopters that swirled above us, blades
thwacking across the dirty sky, cops on bullhorns

leaning into the night, shouting *That's enough,*
time to go home . . .

And so, a trail of headlights snaking out of the pits,
back onto the paved road, to the parking lot at Taco

Bell where once, I got so wasted I forgot my face
was plastered all over the *Bakersfield Californian*

just that morning for some unmemorable volleyball
achievement, and a cop found me lolling

across the asphalt in a stupor, in search of a bean
burrito, and asked what I had been doing earlier

that night—which was, at the time, what I did
every night I wasn't forced out of town, to the bright

and painfully calm sea. Being incoherently
drunk, I happily answered, *That's none of your business,*

officer, to which the cop replied, *I could arrest you*
for being drunk in public (which I thought was a little

extreme), until he tilted his head to once side and took
what seemed like an unnecessarily long look at me

and said, *I know who you are, you were in the paper*
this morning for getting a full-ride to play back

*East; my daughter plays for Garces, she would die
to be you* (which I thought was a little extreme) . . .

If I didn't know who you were, he continued,
I'd throw you in jail,

and something in me wished he would;
somehow I wanted *proof* of how terrible I felt

my life had become, and here was this man
who could give it to me but was so *unwilling.*

He let me drive home drunk and sneak back
into my room with the Laura Ashley wallpaper

and matching comforter, under which I woke
the next morning naked and bruised with thorns

stuck in my thighs and ass from falling down
one of the dirt foothills—I suppose—

although it all seemed so unclear, my door flying
open, my father's voice booming across the room,

opening the blinds, saying, *You can't just lie in bed
all day,* at seven o'clock in the morning;

somehow I wanted proof
of how terrible I felt my life had become

in Bakersfield, this harsh, unshakable voice
crashing through my dirt life, telling me it was time

to clean the house, *You know what they say—
Cleanliness is next to Godliness, Get up, Get up, Get up* . . .

RICHES

There were things to be thankful for, like the silver-blue
Porsche with the black leather bra strapped over the headlights
and parked in the two-car garage, next to the leased
diesel Mercedes that clanged down the street like a bucket

of spoons; and there were places to go the afternoon my mother
walked out on my father after twenty-five years.
He and I were fighting, as usual, only this time I screamed
I can't take it, I'm leaving—

and began throwing things into a suitcase, including a flask
of vodka I kept on the top shelf in my closet. That's when my mother
walked into my room and said in a certain flatness,
I'm going with you . . .

and we got in the car and started driving. My brother
was riding home on his bicycle when my mother pulled over
and rolled down the window, *Your sister and I are leaving,*
she said, *Go home and see your father—*

(This moment, my grandmother swears,
ruined my brother's life.) My grandmother was home,
baking a boysenberry cobbler when we pulled up to her house;
I flew out of the car and darted across the lawn covered in pink

Albizia blossoms, into the warm kitchen
and eventually, my grandmother's floured arms.
She pressed my head against her apron and held me
for I don't know how long—*years*

could have passed in that moment,
as my mother wobbled into the room, slow as sunlight,
falling with us in a heap of sobbing on the warm linoleum,
and her father, my grandfather, entering in silence,

leaning against the wall, head hung like a broken flower,
hands in worn out pockets. That night, there were fresh,
cool sheets on the guest bed in the *blue room,*
my grandmother called it,

and trembling shadows on the walls of the sewing room
the next morning when I woke up from this *horrible dream*
where life as I knew it was over; where I caused—
I felt like I caused the end of my parents' marriage,

and there was coffee gurgling in the kitchen, the scent
of roasted earth wafting through the house that was not my
house, into the bedroom that was not my bedroom,
which meant there was no dream; this was my *life . . .*

TRUCK

The best part about my mother dating
other men after she left my father
was that I no longer had to stay home
and watch her drink wine out of a box

in the kitchen, or watch her sit and stare
at the TV in the dark, in her underwear
and one of my volleyball T-shirts
with my name and number ironed on

the back; my name that was no longer
her name. When she was home
with John, I could finally be *alone*
which I could never otherwise be

because of the *guilt* of my mother
leaving my father, "Because the two
of you were fighting, he was trying
to control you and you weren't having it;

he wouldn't let you leave the house
or do anything with your friends;
You weren't *free;*
you were *destroying yourself*"—

I'm not sure if John the truck driver
had a last name. He was much shorter
than my mother, drove an eighteen-wheeler,
drank Budweiser, and smoked packs

of unfiltered Marlboro cigarettes
he kept in the freezer in the house—
which meant I could smoke and drink
in the house

which meant I was *free*,
and no longer had to pretend I wasn't
destroying myself. John had a tan left arm,
"From the way I drive, see—I lean like this

out the window," and when he came over,
my mother started wearing lipstick again,
and listening to Buck Owens on KUZZ
FM radio, wearing plaid shirts

"To look like more of a cowboy,"
or at least a cowboy's girlfriend.
"I always hated those dresses and heels
your father made me wear; I never did like it—

wasn't me." I wasn't so sure who she was
anymore, this woman, or who I was either;
her dresses and heels no longer fit me, but
neither did the flannel shirts with pearled

buttons, or the Wranglers with yellow stitching
swirled on the butt she picked off the racks
at Goodwill and Salvation Army on Union
Avenue and took back when things went bad

with John, along with my volleyball jerseys
with her old name, *my name*, ironed on
the back; but the idea that I could smoke
and drink openly, in the house, with

or without her, as much as I wanted—
needed to, is what kept me alive
long enough to get out of Bakersfield;
is what remained.

OLEANDER

At my father's wedding, the vague
memory of two glasses on the dinner table;—

a goblet and flute for each guest, a bottle
of red wine on the left, white on the right, champagne
in the center—for the toast,
                              —if you wished.

I always wished.

This was like heaven. This was like living was
possible . . .

I swished the delicate globes in my hand and tossed warm
crimson rivers down my throat while people ate dinner,—

                    I would imagine,

            —though I wasn't aware of it at the time
but why wouldn't they? This was something
alright; this was *cause*
            for celebration . . .

Then, hours later,
the room swollen with music, bodies rising
and floating on the dance floor like ripped photographs
            swirling down a toilet,—

if I closed one eye and kept the other open,
I could make out a large figure standing below the disco ball,
now turning,
now signaling in slow, silent motions for me to

Come on, Come out here,
Come dance
with your father:—

and I thought, Oh
no—
he's talking to *me*,

Then suddenly: remembering I no longer existed
according to the Catholic Church
which issued the annulment,

The one thing (*the only thing?*)
he loved so hard he crushed it,

and thank God for that warm, sweet nectar
rolling around my stomach
that gave me enough courage to laugh,
shake my head back and forth and
refuse

while his new wife scurried into his arms,
while hundreds of guests stared in confused disapproval
as I staggered out the door

and into my car, my father
rushing into the sweltering parking lot in his tuxedo
in what could have been tears,
screaming, *Where are on earth
are you going?*

But I was already gone,
swerving down Highway 178 in the fast lane
beside hulking oleanders dividing me and oncoming traffic,

their branches shaking in the fevered wind,
tossing their hot pink petals

into the open lanes.

DESCENT

You have to follow the path of your blood.
—Garcia Lorca

I began in the San Joaquin Valley
beneath my grandmother's blood-
red cherry tree, my mother's bed
of wild mint and climbing rose.
We fed on tri-tip and pork-chops and
barbecued chicken, ate my grandfather's
homemade fudge with goblets of Uncle Joe's
homemade wine. My aunt Donna burned
every variety of cookie she ever made.
My dad was a poor man who managed
a trucking company and often screamed.
He married my mom before she discovered
he was in debt. Who could blame him
for seeing the cash registers in her eyes.
She worked at Reese Oil Company,
Western Stockman's Cattle, Century 21,
while he ate gallons of light
pink strawberry ice-cream.
My whole life has been covered in dirt.
No man ever seemed worth the effort.
I felt nervous until I found a decent ball-
point pen. There is no use in comprehending
the past. With my first breath of freedom
I swallowed a bottle of vodka and moved
to Manhattan. Cockroaches, trash, tattoos.
I'm lasting here like the Bakersfield sun
come August. The one that gave me skin
cancer. My face and body burned there
for eighteen years. No amount of grief
can knock my grandmother's laugh out of me,

or my Aunt Donna; or my mom,
who didn't just turn on the engine
of her leased silver-blue diesel Mercedes.
She drove it through the house.

SPRING

There are no writers in California, my lover said, ninety-six
rejection letters for his first novel stacked upon his crooked desk,
the plot of his second novel—about *cement*—slowly entering
his computer as I depart for LAX. In the last chapter, another woman
lying on his mattress, on dust colored sheets pushed against the wall
where I left handprints, which is how I tell it in Los Angeles,
my first collection of poems due out next Spring.

HUMAN RESOURCES

Why Jennifer instead of Nora, the name
I always wanted like the girl in *Pete's Dragon*
who sang while the tide washed inside of secret caves.

At work, the Human Resource lady says I've
been a bitch most of March. I said, March
was a long month, a bag of dog shit splattered

on Sullivan Street, a homeless man eating
pizza on the 2 train headed downtown, eight months
after I found out I had cancer, eight months

without drinking, scared of everything
I touched, it was enough to shove a frail woman
walking down Spring where everyone seemed worthy

of being punched in the nose or the "noggin"
my grandpa would say, No, I do not think I'm *angry*,
I think of my friend Hernando who said eating on the

train is like eating in the bathroom, yet he wasn't
clean; that *concept* didn't stop him from lighting a blunt
every night after his brother died, driving over the Verrazano

circa 1999, the sky leaking water like paint spilled
on paper by a child locked in a room
who didn't want to be alone

after her parents split the china, divided the dog,
gave weekends to her father who sobbed each time
she backed out of the driveway, smoking Camel Lights

to the soundtrack of *The End of the World*;—
headed toward a canyon where grape tangled with orange
groves, and the groves—the groves formed *finally*

a pattern that made sense; at the time I did not feel
anything, stick-shifting out of my mother's face
in the rearview mirror; crying and longing

and praying for something dark, something damp
like a wave crashing against glass or
perhaps it was the wall of a secret cave.

LILIES

Always the infant artist knocking
the back of your brain at night, saying,
Look at the lilies spreading their pink
legs open pronged, forking out wet
on the window. Look at the oranges on
the corner, ripe and ready to burst
into a thousand seeds. See the bodega
light, always on. Always the asshole
galloping out of your mouth at dinner,
claiming you can play tennis though you
haven't since you were sixteen when you
quit, like you quit all things, always swinging the racket against the shadow
of the ball; tugging your mother's skirt,
wanting what she ordered: not pasta
but fish; not silence but river; not
holding but heaving the arrogant
lilies, attached to the long, hard stem.
Eventually, you find yourself clutching
the umbrella when it hasn't rained
for weeks; before you pick up the pen,
someone better has already begun
writing the story of your life, the character
who turns out to be you, asleep in the T-
shirt that says, *Love Me*. Before seeking
someone to fix, you might want to pull
back the bandage, might want to check on
the scab; before you call the cleaning
lady, change the sheets with flowers and know
that all we touch, we smother. All we

cherish we crush against each other,
fumble through the dark until it slips
to morning. See the rose petals strewn
on the street before you call the doctor,
consider stabbing yourself with a lily,
just to make sure you still bleed.

IRIS

Approaching her twenty-seventh year
the woman walking down 34th Street,
weather mild and Macy's intact,
considers hurling herself out a window.
It's called defenestration, her boyfriend
says. Thanks. However the woman,
(being on the sidewalk) has no window
at that moment and some would call
that moment God. No mother likes
to give cash as a gift, but the daughter
who has ten dollars in the bank and
a twenty-dollar withdrawal minimum
admits receiving a fifty-dollar Starbucks
Card and a bundle of purple silk
does not make an uplifting birthday
experience. The woman gives her mother
a five-hundred dollar balance on a deferred
student loan, which is one way to say
I love you but difficult to find inscribed
in a card. That day, her grandmother falls
into a bed of blue iris. Her grandmother
has since been moved to a nursing home.
Don't worry. Get some rest. Difficulty
sleeping happens when the mind tries
to make truth out of the false, therefore
the woman will sleep if she can just focus
on the truth. When it is Easter she can say
It is Easter It is Easter over and over.
Only if it is Easter and the nurse passes out
giant cookies at her grandmother's

nursing home and her grandmother folds
her one cookie into a napkin,
stashes it in her purse and carries it across
town on a bus to another nursing home
where her husband is dying of Alzheimer's
disease; if she gives it to him
and he doesn't know what the round
thing is; if she helps him chew and swallow
and he doesn't know who *she* is,
never mind the nurse who puts a star
on the back of his wheelchair because
He is great, the nurse says, He is great—
when this kind of truth gets stuck
on the dead branch of the woman's mind
it might not help her sleep
even though it's true. At that point
she might consider saying, It is nighttime.
And it is dark outside. And it is dark
inside. It is dark It is dark It is dark.

BAKERSFIELD

Driving over the Grapevine toward Los Angeles,
I felt for the first time I would be free of my provincial town,
of my past, an oil rig and a broken tractor parked in a ditch
on the side of the highway, acres and acres of dirt,
dry riverbeds and cotton fields, 65 miles an hour behind me.

I was eighteen, and sat in a black Saturn beside my first and only
boyfriend in Bakersfield, a philosophy major at the Community College
who came from Oildale and had a fondness for weed and crystal meth.

I am never coming back, I said,
blowing smoke out the half-cracked window, into the blistering
brown air. I had never listened to jazz. Or seen the valley's cracked floor
covered in snow. *You'll be glad to be from a farm town
once you're away,* my boyfriend said with plain confidence.

A decade later I shudder to think of that last drive out of the San
Joaquin,
my single mother waving goodbye from the front porch,
barefoot behind the giant pine, beside pots of geraniums,
the different states and time zones that would grow between us,
the years,
now each of us at peace in her own private winter,
landscapes we endured and called *home.*

PERPETUAL HELP

There's no way of explaining faith,
or the way it surfaces like a corpse
in your childhood river, changing
your perspective on the once fresh water
that soothed your burnt summer skin.

How can you not believe?
You plant a Siberian elm to document
what was lost, and take from its absence the fondest
story, which you saved for a man
you never dreamed would arrive,
and you weep through the night in his arms
to feel you were not in danger
that faith saved its most severe hour
for you alone.

Faith is the other life you never
knew existed, the one that opens like a blanket
on the grassy hill, that bends like the young
maple, answers the faint knock at the door
where a despairing girl finds you
asleep in your lover's bed
as you so often are
during the hours of your sorrow.

It comes to the student at her desk.
It comes to the man emptying trash
with his hands, to the child
whose drunken father just stumbled home.

It comes to the infidel, to the cat eating
a box, to the dealer, to the shoplifter,
and to the dishwasher rinsing cups through the night.
       It even comes to the dirt
in the endless fields of poppies
to rain falling on an abandoned barn,
to the body, tired of bearing its life.

MYSORE

A barefoot man wrapped in a lavender *doti*
pushing a cart of zucchini and spinach
down a swarming dirt road, screaming,
"Vegetables, vegetables, vegetables."

My grandfather in his life never raised
his voice or hand against any of his children.
He worked on the Pacific Coast Railroad,
trains that snaked up and down

California's knotted shoulders. On weekends,
he drank tea and played harmonica. Something
in the absence of his voice as he stared at the orange
blossoms told me he longed for his old life

in Ireland, though he would never dream of leaving
my grandmother and returning home, or travelling
to India, like I did. "Hot there," is all he would say
if he could, shaking his white head with a grin

sweeter than sugar. When he was scattered
across the earth like paper, I flew across the world
and landed in Bangalore, then took a four hour taxi
to Mysore. The villagers were dark and lank. The men

squatted beside demolished shacks and burning
piles of trash, selling chai and jasmine to string into
garlands. The women wore orange and pink and neon
violet saris, beat their laundry against rocks, carried baskets

of branches, children, jugs of water. Kids laughed
as they lugged bricks of mud and spread them across
the earth like winning hands of cards. White cranes
speckled the rice paddy fields where sunlight fell

in pools of water. I sat in the blue interior of a white
Ambassador driven by a man who was less than half
my size. A beaded rosary with a silver Jesus swung
from the rearview mirror, his divine arms speared

to the figurative wooden cross. I stared at his bare metal feet
swinging back and forth as the car hurled itself over
the deeply pitted road. I could be wrong, but it seemed like Jesus
was dancing to the Indian music oozing out of the radio,

voices crooning the names of a thousand Hindu Gods,
praising them for this or that job, or love, or life.
And for one moment, I had no desire. I didn't want
to be anyone else. Or anywhere else in the world.

II. LIP

MEANTIME

Before the CIA murdered Fred Hampton
he used to say to his wife Akua
Tell me I am a revolutionary
before I fall asleep.

I think of him shot dead that night
and remind myself I don't need
what the masses do not have,
which means I don't want much.

I don't want to put my money in banks
to be double charged for my withdrawals,
don't want shoes, belts or jackets
made from another's skin,

don't want to see my words on movie screens
produced by low-wage hands;
I don't want to sleep
in my warm bed in peace

until the junkie on my doorstep is clean,
and in the meantime, I *know*
what they know and won't tell me
in the *New York Times*.

Lately, I don't want to walk in female feet.
I'm sickened by the beauty they sell me—
I don't want a flat stomach,
straight hair, smooth legs—

I don't want to confine my breasts to underwire
or decorate my backside with expensive silk
panties; I know Victoria's Secret,
and it's not worth telling.

*

And I'm telling you for my own good
I don't want you anymore.
I don't want to long for you
with each turn of my ticking clock

or think of how you held me,
how we locked like tangled bicycles
after a deadly crash—
I no longer wish

for days without rain
that remind me of home
in the California sunshine, days
so warm they burned spots on my skin

with heat and love, no—
I don't want to remember you anymore,
or how I felt the first time you kissed me
and opened my heart:

I remember it—the one I used to own,
but now that I've grown so wise, so cold,
I don't want anymore quiet nights alone
and I don't want to be so far from home.

*

I want to peel the city sidewalk back,
rip the concrete off Houston, downtown,
and lay my tired body down on bare, gritty
New York City dirt.

I want to lift something too heavy,
like drunk men. Take them out of the Bowery
and build them a home, lend them my hands
so they know they aren't alone;

I want to raid too-cool vintage shops,
give their marked-up, dressed-down,
fucked-up merchandise back
to Salvation Army where it belongs,

and on a good day, I want all the men
I pass on the street to keep staring at my breasts
until they turn into fists that fly off me
and whack them on lips that bleed

the blood of my woman being.
I want my bladder to grow so large
I can drink the Atlantic without peeing,
absorb salt and vomit rainwater
into mouths of thirsty children.

*

I want to crawl up
inside my tired grandmother's body
and stretch out my youth within her,
then tumble that sweet girl around

and around on blue carpet,
do cartwheels on tulips and dance
on smoldering rocks—
I want to run her ragged,

until she's exhausted and sleeps
like a newborn baby in my arms;
I don't want much really,
I don't want much at all.

AMADOU'S NEW YORK

"Shooting him is murder. Shooting him 41 times is discrimination"
—Amadou Diallo's father

- Because the ocean is selling thirst.
- Because the sun is selling cancer.
- Because the moon is selling America.
- Because the university is selling debt.
- Because the sex shop is selling Disney.
- Because the street is selling sleep.
- Because the president is selling faith.
- Because the frame shop is selling guns.
- Because the juice bar is selling hash.
- Because the bar is selling cocaine.
- Because the theater is selling tears.
- Because the gallery is selling revolution.
- Because the record is selling the past.
- Because the cigarette is selling slavery.
- Because the razor is selling rabbits.
- Because the mirror is selling light.
- Because the alcoholic is selling God.
- Because the doctor is selling fear.
- Because the lawyer is selling truth.
- Because the landlord is selling nothing.
- Because the psychiatrist is selling grief.
- Because the divorcee is selling romance.
- Because the child is selling his parents.
- Because the saint is selling sex.
- Because the poet is selling the spirit.
- And the spirit is the woman.
- And the woman is the music.
- And the music is the magic.
- And the magic has been lost.

- Because the cops are selling the beat.
- Because the beat is selling the bullets.
- Because the bullets are selling blood.
- Because the blood is selling the heart.
- Because the heart is wrapped in skin.
- Because the skin is selling a gift.
- Because that gift was taken.
- Because that gift was life.
- Because the beat is time.
- It never stops.
- It never stops.
- It never stops.

POSITIVE

you cannot fall
in love with a man
who has HIV
she said

you cannot fall
you cannot fall
you cannot fall
in love

he is positive
13 years
he is 32
he is covered in

tattoos
and statistics
and statistics
say

but when he moves
he looks like a
living painting
he looks

like the ceiling
of the Sistine
Chapel he burns
like shrapnel

in my skin and
HIV and
HIV is
fatal

and so is cancer
and I
am in remission
and it

could come back and
kill me this life
is fatal and one
could be hit

by a taxi
or my fist
flying across this
candlelit table

and he
could be alive
for another
13 years

HAIKU TO KNOCK 10 YEARS
OFF YOUR MOTHER'S LIFE

I called to say I
stopped eating meat and sometimes
I sleep with women

DIFFÉRANCE

All your friends are going back to school,
going back to NYU to learn to write
limericks. And you will still be here—
wiping your ass with downy metaphors,
whoring stories of lovers you don't even have.

You will still be dreaming of Marcuse
sitting on a beach in post-capitalist heaven,
teaching Angela Davis how to smash in
windows and meanwhile, the dentist says,

you've been grinding your teeth at night.
You've been holding your breath in the shower,
shaving your legs with a razor tested for safety
on the whites of wide-eyed rabbits, so what
do you do? You ask for a miracle.

Ask for a miracle and you just might get it.
Next thing you know, Todd Colby
is sitting next to you at a radio station,
talking about Derrida
as though you don't know the *différance*

between Karl Marx and Carl's Junior—
as though you didn't spend a hundred grand
in graduate school just to hear Yeshitela
lecture on the impact of your skin
in Hyde Park and Kenwood,

as if you've been sitting on your ass
watching Ali Macbeal pretend not to be
anorexic. Turns out you cannot be alone
with a box of brownies. You're acting
like Gandhi reborn on East Thirteenth Street—

I don't think so. You may be a child of God
but you are also second child of a woman
who never wanted a second child and no,
you do not want to be the next Sylvia Plath,
sticking your head in the oven over love

or lack thereof, also known as Ted Hughes.
So what do you do? You run. You run
to New York City surprised to find
you've brought yourself with you
to a world where poetry and women
are undervalued and guess what—

you are both. You can change the poet part
but the vagina will be difficult to edit out.
But miracles do happen. And one day
someone sees you on the street and screams

Poet! Next thing you know the blind
man at the back of the bar has memorized
all of your lines and screams into the midnight
sky, *Don't give me none of that old shit—*
you better be bad!

He thinks you've been in California all this time,
visiting your grandma who blames you for leaving,
What a shame she says, What a shame.
What a shame you never learned how to cook.
What a shame you've been in bed for six months,

trying to slit your wrists without bleeding,
dreaming of impaling your body on gates
of Gramercy Park as an embodied metaphor
of class division, thinking I am not the next
Nina Simone. I am the skim milk of Allen
Ginsburg. I live in a room the size of an egg-

plant, my parents are threatening to visit
and I've been having nightmares of standing
on stage in front of three-hundred *black*
revolutionaries, knowing full well my grandpa
is the cause of their suffering,

knowing he's from Dublin
And you know what they say about the Irish,
Jenny. The Irish are the niggers of Europe.
Grandpa's talking like he knows
and you're acting like you've been there
when the closest you got was a bottle of gin.

You've been trying to Clorox the freckles off your skin
thinking you're not good enough when the truth is—
the truth is in the moment. And at the moment
Barnes and Noble is out of Tolstoy's
The Kingdom of God is Within You.

Barnes and Noble is out of Tolstoy,
the kingdom of God is within you
and you want to marry an urban cowboy
who carves your name in the moon
and paints your toes

the color of blood, the color of love
the color of what colonialism might look like—
it might look something like you: a poster
of a painting of a portrait of a woman

by Klimt hanging on every freshman dorm
on this side of the Western Hemisphere

where all your friends are going back to school
and yes, you will still be here
but guess what—here is home,
here is eternity, here is where
you belong,

so let the voice roll off your tongue
and act as if art could change you,
take you out of yourself
into another world, a better world,
there must be.

LIFE CAFÉ

Next to me last night, the boy I loved last
summer. The blonde, the actor, the one
who went crazy is the way we remember
him now. Not the hero in the *Invention
of Love*, not the child molester on *Law
and Order*, six-foot-two, body like
sculpture, Michelangelo's David
in Tompkins Square Park. One August
night he drove out of Manhattan,
into a forest in Connecticut where
he got naked, beat his chest, and begged
the Virgin Mary, *Mary I love you, Mary,
name me the son of God; I am Jesus,
I am your son*. I'm not sure what Mary did,
but his parents put him in the hospital.
He stayed in paper slippers and watched
September 11th on TV. I saw him one week
after and he said he knew it was going to happen—
in hindsight, he predicted the whole thing.
He said Mary drove him out of the city
and he was saved. A year later he sat
beside me in a church basement and said
there was a strange energy returning
to the city and he wanted to acknowledge
it because his phobias were coming back:
spiders crawling up his arms. Patches of dark.
Living in a tunnel only unlike last year
he is able, he thinks, to see the light.

FALL, NEW YORK

My eyes have seen steel crumble like sand
and orchids last in a vase without water
for more than a week. Now, how am I to
reconcile death with what continues living?
Ash lifts like confetti from the sewer,
tanks sink inside the Hudson River.
They barricaded the park last night
but I know the trees are out there shimmering,
doing their thankless work; I know the branches
must grow tired of holding up all that life;
the leaves keep changing their minds—
they want to be green then red then brown,
and who can blame them for wanting to fall
and throw themselves like open hands
upon the warm unbroken ground.

STORIES OFF THE EARTH

I call my grandmother at the nursing home in south-
west Bakersfield to tell her I survived the World
Trade Center falling, fire blooming like hot, neon
petals of Iceland poppies in the backyard of my childhood
house on Christmas Tree Lane. Do you remember
that house? I say. "Oh of course I do, for Chrissake—
how old do you think I am? Do you remember?
Do you remember your mother? When are you going
to move back home?" I tell her Nancy saw men
in three-piece suits leap from windows eighty
stories off the earth. She says, "Courage comes like faith
comes to those who need it first, and then to those who work;
that stranger things have happened than seeing humans fly.
And why don't you get a job, by the way? You're too old
to be floundering. You do realize that, don't you?
That you're too old to be floundering?" I tell her the air
I breathe contains dirt and ash and burns the back
of my throat and may contain asbestos.
She says, "Well your high-school had asbestos,
and your mother's house had asbestos, and your Aunt
Donna's house had asbestos too, so I wouldn't worry
about that too much. Plus," my grandmother says,
"you already had cancer and survived that. Do you really
think God would give you the same lesson twice?"

JIMMY

*

Memories flash like glittering crosswalks
ignited on Pacific Coast Highway,

on a corner where a man stops traffic
while walking toward the sea.

I in my life have moved

as far East as possible,

and back

*

to California, my adolescent house,
my grandmother's voice on the phone, her TV
singing in the background, Oprah Winfrey
afternoon afternoon.

I just want to die,
my grandmother says.

Broken elbow, crooked hip,
too much flesh on the bone.

If you want to die, you probably won't,
the saying goes . . .

She is not dying from the passing of Hugh,
her husband, or the sixty-five years
they were married, or the mere three
months he has been gone.

At night I can feel someone
holding my hand;—

I knows it's him,

She tells me this while I sit on the edge of her bed
next to the memory of the black cat she gave back to the vet
because she felt the cat was despondent sitting all day long
in one room with mint-green walls, blue light of the television
beaming in darkness as night falls and my grandmother fails to rest.

Do you think you will stay here? she asks, *Do you miss it*
back East? And then:

*

Go find me the black pill.
Don't ever get this old. It's a horrible thing.

*

On September 11, 2004, reading the *New York Times*,
waiting in line at a coffee shop in California
when a man behind me leans over and says,

You must be an intellectual.

Two years and two days after I still cry
in the morning still wake up sobbing
torn plane wings still flying through
my dreams—

I remember seeing Jimmy in line at the Korean deli on Spring Street
two years and two days ago, buying a case of beer after not having
drank in ten.

Jimmy cannot get back. Jimmy are you out there? Jimmy
I will always look you in the eye no matter what you're doing,

Jimmy what are you doing—you can't just sleep outside. You are
not a bad man, Jimmy you are not doing anything wrong
it is just that once, as my friend says, you let go of the balloon
it goes sailing on into the never-ending sky
and you spend the rest of your life trying to get it back.

* *

You must be homesick for New York,
my grandmother says, *It's only natural.*

* *

The symptoms are apparent. Shutting
the blinds. Turning the off the lights. Cooking
kale over a rolling boil adding ginger to tofu while I ache
for the city that will never be the same my friends who will never
be the same the acquaintance I lost who will never be the same

and do you remember that day last year

when the wind was a screaming child running down the streets
in Brooklyn because I do. Even the newscasters said,

* *

Ghosts . . .

* *

This year, being in California on the anniversary of it all, I called
my friend Dan the painter in New York to see if there was anything
special about the day and he said he almost forgot it happened. Said
it was just like That September when the weather was so clear and
perfect one believed for a second in a loving God and then he was
shirtless on Ludlow holding a yellow cup of coffee and watching the
second I won't say it tower burn and I was sprinting down Hester
Street toward him and managed for no reason at all to stop and buy
congee from a nameless Chinese restaurant in Chinatown for no
reason other than I wanted something warm inside me just like for

no reason I would imagine Jimmy standing in that line with cans of beer tucked under his arm and then there were the days that bled into months of weeping for no reason except, right, and now there are years.

*

I am writing to say New York is with me, here;
that I will be back. No really—

*

Of course, my grandmother says.
You will probably go back . . .

SWIMMING

We talked about That September
two years later in Laguna,
bobbing in the sea. How they decided
to call it Patriot's Day. How we
remember what we touched
that year we were still living
back in New York: our fingers
dust, our hair a halo of ash. How
to be conscious of the past
soaked in the present lack of history
in Southern California. The waves
kept deafening our speech,
booming and unfurling their tongues
on the hot gold sand where children
tip-toed over pebbles and clapped
and clapped no matter what we said.
No matter, the sea. Kids screaming
as we pulled seaweed out of our bikinis
and wondered how many years
it would take before we got far enough
away from that eastern day and place
to turn tragedy inside out, into a national
holiday of hot dogs and fireworks,
How long will it take us to heal?
We want to know as blankets open
like torn kites upon a happy shore.

GOOD THINGS

And there were good things that came
out of it—the few trains running were
empty because everyone was too scared
to get on the subway so you could
get wherever you needed to go pretty
fast. And all the shoeless homeless
people that normally roamed between
cars selling batteries and blinking key
chains just flat out disappeared,
so you didn't have to look in their
eyes and see they were the same color
as yours and wonder where they slept
when night landed on the city. There was
no more night, no dark. It was a child's
dream of constant light: shining and
shining and shining down on burning
piles of—, and firemen saving, missing,
pillaging. You could walk down the center
of Broadway below Canal Street and not
get killed by a cab or bus or messenger
lugging an industrial bike lock around
his waist, rushing toward the World
Trade Center because now that was—,
and you had to show your photo ID
to the National Guards in neighborhoods
like Little Italy where The Feast of San
Gennaro was canceled; and all the abandoned
festival booths and rides just sat there
collecting ash until finally people gave up
and dismantled them with these . . . gruesome

looks on their faces like they had lost
some deep love they would nevereverever
get back. People were screwing like wild
animals on the *Discovery Channel*
when they weren't watching the news—
you could hear easy moans pouring over
the East River. Bodegas ran out of milk
and bread. Now that was scary—to see
empty brass racks and dust so thick it crept
between your eyelashes and inside cracks
where your gas mask met your face. Bars
made a killing. Cigarettes were smoked.
There were posters of the missing glued
and stuck and nailed and hammered into
every street lamp, traffic signal, bulletin
board, tree. And there were new activities
and things to do. Vigils and prayer circles.
Funerals and candles to light or blow out
or leave burning. Everything burning, on fire,
flesh. You could smell it. For months. And
months. And months. You could sit back
and stare at the Hudson River. Listen to
the soft thwack of police helicopters
swirling through the gloriously clear skies
(such a deep blue). And if you lived
uptown you could be thankful
you weren't downtown and if you were
downtown that you weren't on Wall Street
and if you were on Wall Street that you
weren't in the Towers and if you were
in the Towers, well. That's where the good
things pretty much ended. There was an
infinite stream of trucks lugging heaps
of body parts up the West Side Highway
to the ice-skating rink at Chelsea Piers,
now being used as a morgue. And if you

didn't feel like experiencing any of that—
or anything ever again, for that matter,
you could fall apart in the street. Right there.
In the open. You could cry out and no one
would stop and look at you funny or say
a word or even ask why you were so upset
because everyone was so upset for what
seemed like so long they understood exactly
what you meant without you having to say it.
It was better than poetry, the unspoken.

TOLL

In Crawford, Texas, where President Bush is spending the week,
the White House had no immediate reaction to the stunning toll.
                                        —Reuters, 6 April 2004

I am in the office writing personal e-mail about sex
when my coworker interrupts, calling me over to Look,
she says, Look at the e-mail the government just sent me.
She points at the screen with her finger shaking while I read
that her marine husband's battalion was the one that just got
attacked in Ramadi. There were a lot of U.S. casualties,
the message says. *We don't know exactly how many yet;*
we are identifying the names of the men killed
and will notify family members as soon as we find out.
My friend and her 26-year-old sniper husband moved to Camp
Pendleton from Michigan shortly before he got deployed,
right after he got back from serving in the war in Iraq
last year. Last year, only one person died, my friend says.
I've never gotten an e-mail like this before. I say nothing.
Don't you ever work? the company accountant says, walking
by in his gray shirt and gray slacks and slick black belt.
I think I'm going to be sick, my friend says,
and I go back to my desk and read the breaking
news on ABC, AP, BBC, CBC, CBS, CNN, Fox, MSNBC,
NPR, and Reuters. I know there are human beings
over there, boys like my friend's husband, like my step-
brother in the Air Force who just got back, Americans and Iraqi
civilians losing their lives but I can't find the details
online; I can't find the names of the dead.

FAHRENHEIT

The documentary filmmaker called the President
an idiot, the President called the film a piece of crap,
the critics said both were somewhat right and last night
my girlfriend in Manhattan called sobbing, having paid
ten dollars to watch a grieving mother of a dead soldier

killed in the war in Iraq, after the attacks in New York
that we experienced. She had apparently blocked it all out
until she saw the footage of street scenes in the aftermath,
and that's when it all came back.

It's July. I'm lying on my bed in Laguna Beach,
waiting to go out dancing with a recovering stripper,
watching leaves of the eucalyptus tree dance in the blue
skies outside my window, listening to the river of cars
wash down Pacific Coast Highway.

It's a holiday weekend. It's the summer of attempting
to find relief. The beaches are packed. The 405 North is pregnant.
My old tennis partner and I can't figure out why we feel so
depressed with all this warmth. We like to blame the weather:
"The sun is out, I wish I were dead." This year, terror only danced

with me a little. First in the form of leaving Manhattan
for Orange County. Then with that old cancer problem
appearing and disappearing like a child hiding behind a sheer
curtain. And finally with the company I moved for going bankrupt.
At some point, I had to put war on the back burner
with the reoccurring nightmares of September,

and I walked like a ghost through this unmarked seaside realm,
and wondered if this was hell, and whether I had ever really left
California when I was a girl and built a life for myself
on that eastern island I call home.

It's dusk now. Across the street, the sun is folding over the Pacific Ocean.
I don't have to see it to know. I want my city back. Want to hold its soft,
gigantic face in my hands. Want it all as it used to be—
fierce and light and full of heat.

There are unacceptable things life does to you for no identifiable reason,
and unacceptable things you do to yourself for reasons good
and bad, like trying to bury pain by digging a hole in your own chest,
and planting it there, then watching in amazement
as some wildflower grows.

There are events so horrific, — days so wide and heavy
you have to hurl yourself over them as if they were oceans
and you were a fragile thing impaled on the end of a
benevolent stick. And if, when you open your eyes,

you have breath,
and bit of ground below you (as opposed to over you),
then this is a good thing. And you may even consider
kneeling, and giving it a kiss.

IN THE DREAM WHERE YOU DON'T LOVE HER

You are with your new girlfriend at a party,
and I am there too, though I'm not sure what I'm doing

but the people are attractive
and wasted, and I can't tell if you are like them

or not, only that your girlfriend decides to go to bed
and leaves you, and somehow in the night wet with blurred

lights and bright scarves, everyone winds up in
couples—dragging each other into bathrooms

to make out, tearing into each other on the cream
couch of some odd hotel in the middle of I don't know,

Florida, and I am left alone while you find another
woman who kisses you goodnight and moans,

which I am reading as you must not love
your girlfriend that much if you would cheat on her

in my dream, and between my closed eyes I am still lying
on the floor beside you, watching it all unfold, and I turn

and cover my heart with my hand, which I am interpreting
as it still hurts sometimes, even after so

long, and what if I'm alone for the rest of my life
while the rest of the world fractures into thousands

of hand-held units, then I am awake and running
in place on a treadmill at the gym, watching the TV

mounted on the wall which runs a news story that says
Ecstasy is being investigated as a remedy for fear and

depression in Israel, and an American test group is underway—
and for a sweaty second I wonder if I should volunteer

to be part of it so I could know what fearlessness feels like
in the face of despair: suicide bombing on the Gaza Strip,

twenty children killed when an icy roof collapsed in Russia,
riots in Rwanda, rape at Rutgers—every day, the heart

blown out of the human chest and what's the big deal,
I would say in the cool euphoria; I would be able

to open my eyes and watch horror unfold around me,
it wouldn't bother me one bit.

III. FLAME

TIDE

You find yourself accidentally
in what could be love with your
good friend—good because it was
safe as the ocean Pacific, seaweed
that swished beneath your feet
when you were a kid and it was
summer. You were dumb and awake
hours before even the moon
knew how to roll out the waves,
even the moon knew how to
roll out the tide like a pair of dice,
a pair of sixes. High tide, low tide
it didn't matter back then—
it was a gamble, an act of faith
that made you dive face first
into a sea that shaped you soft
and harmless. A child no longer,
summer blossoms far from New York
City where you become willing
to surrender safety for deeper
waters that promise calm. In silence
you come to a body in which you are
floating, in which you are a bottle
with a message stuck inside you
and the only way to read it and
the only way to see it and
the only way to open is to break.

SONG

A shared fondness for Yann Tiersen. Cat Power
singing *I don't blame you* each morning on the
alarm clock. Yelp of the abandoned cat locked
in the dark corridor across from your apartment;

four months, it was practically nothing. So why can't I
forget? Summer rain, Rivington Street, weekends
spent in the shade of a giant elm, maple, raven ash;
shirtless children leaping barefoot over water archways

and broken hydrants; hours lost in community gardens:
fountains, rocks, sun-soaked benches where we guessed
names of flowers within our reach—zinnia, larkspur, climbing
rose. Lilies in a blue vase on your windowsill for my birthday,

sap holding the stamen's powder intact. Handmade
notes you crafted out of vintage postcards and paper bags.
Days like poems, metered and broken, all metaphoric:
the city's heave and collapse, your Super drinking

Old English out of a paper bag on your stoop at noon
while we ride our antique bikes through the East Village
to buy chocolate-chip cookies; a gathering of men twirling
women around their snapping fingers, dancing salsa,

Spanish radio screaming and laughing in front of the Projects
while we watch *Army of Darkness* in the silence
of your rent-controlled apartment. Time to leave
or reasons to stay?

Four months: one-hundred and twenty days. I promised
I would only be gone for a month and never came back.
You found a new girl three weeks after I left. Cat Power
singing *I don't blame yo*u each morning on the alarm clock,

yelp of the abandoned cat. If it were love, it would have
lasted? It was a bad thing because it fell apart so fast?
It doesn't count or it was the closest I got to rapture
in the last ten years of my life.

LOFT

You have long since left this loft,
this brick and mortar building of our past,
the door of last year open to a city
where I sit, stirring water into a bowl
of cake mix for your birthday
when you call to say you've had a girlfriend
for five months but couldn't tell me
because we work together—*Surprise!*
I'm fine, fine I said over the gray phone,
the phone you used to dial my number
when you were a C+ in Human Sexuality,
you were a pack of Newports on a rainy day,
loved me more than your Public Enemy
poster, walked through snow banks
to buy me yellow tulips. I said I'm fine,
cried into the batter, gave up sugar,
and watched your blonde girlfriend—
who is older, who is wiser, who is shorter
than me stick a fork in my dessert.
We're ex's anyway; we haven't had sex
in over a year—no. I haven't had sex
in over a year—you've been getting off
under cover, covers in the loft, probably
in the same bed where you bought me a pink,
glittered dildo and I said you're going
to have to find another socket to stick that
thing in, and I guess you did. Things change.
I understand. But I haven't forgotten the day
you found out I had cancer and cried
like a lost child on the first day of school,

fell into my arms like a spoon against a bowl
and took me to Zen Palate. Over brown rice
you said you didn't believe in God, that for you,
God meant nature, green and good like broccoli.
It meant electricity—you can't see it or touch it
with your hands, but it's in everything, you said.
It's like Prego, it's in there, and somehow
I thought that sounded *profound*. The idea
that when the body dies something else keeps
living. I haven't deleted the e-mail you sent last
week where we fall in love again. We get married
on an island in Greece. We grow extremely tall
children and if it's a boy, you say, he'll be in
the NBA and make millions, and if it's a girl
she will what? She'll fall in love with a man
who prefers boxed cake? No. She'll sit alone
in a loft somewhere between SoHo and hell? No.
I've already done it for her. I've already blown up
your washer. Packed it in too full, so full
it caught fire so I pulled the plug but the smoke
kept coming in clouds that tasted electric.

BANKER

The date with the investment
banker didn't go well like most dates
I go on don't go well, not in the case
of something tragic happening like Mark's
ex-girlfriend struck by a bus on Canal Street,
tossed off her bike like a Frisbee. We sat in
the lamplight at Café Reggio drinking coffee
that tasted like mop water while he told
a story about how he got drunk in Greece
and rented a scooter: "I threw up
my hands and raced like Tom Cruise
in *Top Gun*—Do you remember that scene?"
I nodded but recalled nothing but Ice Man
playing volleyball on the beach. In Greece,
the banker raised his drunk hands and crashed
and fell off the scooter and luckily (pause)
luckily he was fine but the bike scattered
like confetti and he carried the broken
frame over his shoulder like a lovesick girl.
He gave it to the Greek bike shop owner
who spent all of his time polishing and wiping
and shining up bikes. At that point I had to go
to the bathroom but the riveting story kept
me in place. When the banker approached
with the dismembered bike the Greek man's
hands took to his face like a nurse takes
to an invalid, like pain the body remembers,
handlebars striking the scull. The jolted
Greek went to his desk and cursed
in a language the banker didn't speak

and the banker—my date—was thinking
thousands, how many thousands he would
owe for the drinking accident when the owner
looked up and said, "Two hundred dollars."
I thought I could go to the bathroom at that point
but alas, the story was not over. A party started
inside the banker whose eyes flickered like
cockroach wings because he knew in Greece,
you are always supposed to bargain. So he
licked his lips and looked the man dead
in the eye and said, "I'll give you five dollars
for it." Just then, a funeral started inside me.
I began weeping which was odd
because I didn't know the woman who died.
I tried to keep the dirges down, the bagpipe
players quiet in their kilts while the smiling
banker told me how the Greek man cried
like a teething child. That moment I thought
about the not-bad possibility of being scooped
off the earth in a flash, flung like a compact disk
into the air and shot into a thousand songs—
the body no more, or less, when it lands
than a scattering of broken music, a girl's
sweet voice ricocheting off the streets

CLEMENTINE

It was her first date in over a year without drinking,
he was a professor, she was hopeful, thought often

of what might happen—like tulips in plastic longing to be
unwrapped. *I offer this to you*, he would say, like a priest

offers Christ. They would cross the West Side Highway, romp
through grass at midnight, stare at Venus next to the World

Trade Center. There would be a wedding in Rome, the coliseum
enough to water the eyes. And there would be good times

to talk about, times like the first time he took her *for coffee,*
he said, as they walked down broken sidewalk on West Eleventh

when a cab barreled toward them and he pushed up against her
and she thought, *My Hero*, and he said, I *was trying to save*

myself. (The way she once veered toward the edge of the road
closest to where her father sat while he taught her how to

drive). When he said *coffee* he meant *my apartment;* poster
of Kafka hung on the wall next to Maggie the cat that

disliked her. He offered her an orange that was really a
clementine. It even had a sticker. And she sat there

sucking, spitting on paper, on carpet that smelled like cat
shit next to the table of cigarette butts and empty

bottles of St. John's Wort, silent but wanting to bellow
out, *This is not an orange. This is not an orange. This is not*

an orange. It was the first time she told the truth about her
past; the angry father, the absent brother, the mother

going bankrupt by Edward's Air Force Base. There. She said it.
And nothing broke. Not even Kafka watching the Lakers

lose. Not even bookshelves full of canonical references
she kept missing. *You don't know who Galway Kinnell is? Gal-*

*way Kinnell? He was Big I mean Big I mean as Big as
it gets.* And for the first time I don't know was the best answer

on West Sixteenth, next to the bathroom with a big tub where
she wanted to sink the screenwriter who showed her his short-

short film that won the Berlin something-or-other award,
dropped his pants in the first five minutes of her first first date,

explained he was hot in the dark of his room and kissed her
for the last time in her first year without a drink.

CANVAS

First time I saw you I didn't see
shooting stars in the sky, fireworks
in July, bombs in the dark of my
eyelids. I saw short. Five-foot-six, okay
seven, maybe eight on a good day
or a leap year. You were a low-hung
hotel shower spraying my torso
with so little water it felt like
being spit on. Your skin—not charcoal
black, not brown, not coffee roasted dark
or green, even as olives smashed to
a pulp in Little Italy. It
was *Off Off* Broadway, white as canvas
before a painting. I didn't see
sunshine, no rain, no Brooklyn-Bridge swaying
blues guitar playing hands tangled like
basket handles, like branches of sun
turning dust to daylight stars or something equally miraculous; you
were all cotton, crimson, cut-off shorts,
and I saw the canvas again, light
of your skin covered in ink. You were
a living painting, a chunk of the
Sistine Chapel, you were practical:
remembered my name. And I remembered
little things that stuck to me over
the years like gum sticks to a shoe. Your
hair of dirt and earth and soil became
simple as a seed falling to the ground
becomes a bed of roses, becomes

a whole new way of being in the
world for the first time I thought, Perhaps
God does exist. Perhaps he or she
or it knew. I couldn't take anymore
surprises, no more knights in shining
armor, no more volts of lightening through
this swollen heart, and so he gave it
to me slow as ice-cream melting in
a bowl becomes a pool of light or
something equally miraculous.

PORTRAIT OF THE ARTIST DAN WITZ

He sticks a fly sticker on my key,
sticks hummingbirds, *Life-size,* he says,
on buildings and doorways, paints shadows
below them on Ludlow and although
I've only known him since June, I love
him something awful like swallowing
hair; like one loves a purple T-shirt
with holes. You should really throw that
away but you save it for later,
for someday you might need a rag
that says Mitchell, South Dakota,
Corn Capital of the World. Drunk frat
boys stumble down Orchard to piss
on his door. Only bleach will remove
the smell. The cops keep trying to
arrest him for trespassing. I never
thought I'd fall for a 45-year-old
Jewish man who hates broccoli,
even though he's never tried it.
Something about his mother.
Something about his face makes me
fear living alone. He takes a woman
he claims to love on a date to a cardboard
box spread out like a blanket below
the Williamsburg Bridge. I love him
though I'm not sure how. Like Patrick Swayze
in *Dirty Dancing* or a dirty uncle
you find attractive but would never say.
I like to say his first name fast with his
last so it sounds like sandwich. He told

the woman his ultimate sexual
fantasy: to be completely in love
with one woman, come inside her and hope,
more than anything she gets pregnant.
Her pupils dilated, but that's not why
he said it. He said it because it's true.
She was supposed to leave town for the weekend but she decided to stick around.
Keep that line, he said, you never know,
someday, you might be able to use it.

MOTORCYCLE

After months of nothing between us
except board games on the hardwood
floor of the old house on Livingston,
pixie-sticks at the movies, glances
across the bar you tended with green
dreadlocks and broken ribs; where
you gave me a free pitcher of beer
one night and I finally got drunk
enough to meet you at an afterhours
party. Too unsteady to walk, some guy
threw me over his shoulder and carried
me toward you. At the party I leaned
against the wall awhile. When it was time
to go you drove me down rain-soaked
streets on the back of your motorcycle.
We pulled into your house. I remember
walking past a poster of Joan Jett
on the refrigerator. Wood floors, rain.
Sitting on the edge of your bed flipping
through magazine articles on snowboarding
you had written. Then your body naked,
splayed out, asleep beside me after
what I wished for so long came to pass.
Feeling my way through the dark
in a blackout, slipping on tobacco-
stained clothes, closing the door
to your room. I can still feel the cold
doorknob in my hand. Slabs of sunlight on the kitchen floor. Could not
figure out how to unlatch the back door

to let myself out. Panicked. Climbed
out the the window and fell into a pile
of wet leaves. That was my life back then.
It could have been summer. Or winter.
Syracuse or Chicago. It happened in New
York. It took six years to look back
on the moment I held you then left you
to rest, walked down Westcott Street and
crept up the stairs to my room in the attic
with bats. That summer, the girls
climbed in and out of my bed, stroked
my hair and tried to sooth me. I couldn't
move. Watched the bats circle the arched
ceilling in search of fruit. I don't know
if they ever found any, but every time
I closed my eyes for the next six years
I felt my arms around your waist your
hands on my face that winter no spring
it must have been summer night.
Eight years later I forget the season
but still hear motorcycles in my sleep.

HUNGRY CHARLIE'S

I was the kind of girl who would leave you
in the hospital
down the road from Faegan's Pub

where I got drunk as snow fell out of the putty sky,
and if someone asked how you were
while I was at the bar,

I would order a pint of Killian's Irish Red
and tell them I heard you kept down Jell-O,
therefore, it was a good day.

And then I would wait
for it to be over.

                              *

Two years later,
at your funeral in the campus chapel, your professor father
a book with a broken spine, your mother a folded umbrella
tired of fighting off rain.

In a pew a few rows down,
a man I slept with in a blackout, then blamed,
then ran away from

at the time I ran away.

Consequently, I do not feel
like remembering him either.
Or his canary T-shirt
with a screaming man's face.

He was my favorite bartender
at our favorite bar—

*

Hungry Charlie's,
where you and I spent semesters sitting at tables
in that damp and sunless room, eating popcorn, spilling
beer, carving our names into rotten wood like passengers
marking their place on a sinking ship.

The bartender gave me a pocket-sized bottle of vodka
for my twentieth birthday.

I'll never forget.

This was before you had a cough
we thought was the flu. For a long time
we thought you had the flu.

Then somehow, summer.

*

The old house on Livingston, that basketball player
JB Reafsnyder who lived with me and the girls
but never paid rent—

who sat with his size-fourteen sneakers reeking
in front of the TV set,
playing video games the entire month of August.

Each evening,
his mouth open his fingers on the trigger.

One afternoon the bartender
came over to visit and sat beside me on the plaid couch

rescued from the gutter but I had a hard time looking
him in the eye sober, light

falling through the dirty windows. It was hard enough
to sit beside him in the dark folds of night at Chuck's
as I slogged through sidewalks of black ice
between your hospital bed and my stool at the bar,
no wait . . .

—that isn't right;

it was summer—

I never left the bar never slogged through snow.

Heard you were still in the hospital, didn't go. Sat in the corner
drunk every Sunday for a year where they had free carrots
and cheese to go with the beer.

I was the kind of girl who would leave you to die
in the hospital down the road, throw down

a pint on the house for *me,* the girl
whose friend was dying of Leukemia.

                             *

You didn't make it through.

That was the summer before I drove through Boston
at two in the morning to meet you at a party in Watertown.

You were not sick yet.

You did not have that endless cough that was not the flu;
I had not yet left the bartender who had not yet left town.

*

Then we were out of summers.

We were out of school and you were gone
and the bartender was gone
and I was gone,
though I didn't know that yet—

not until I put the drink down
three years later,

*

When,

*

one day in April I was walking in the rain down Second Avenue
at five o'clock in the evening and bent like a wire hanger
on the sidewalk and all I could think of was you so

I called the girl I drove through Boston to see you with that time
we thought you had the flu and she said it was the anniversary
of your death.

That day.
Three years

*

later. My body remembered what used to be your life
always beside me during those endless upstate winters
for two years when I could have gone to see you in the hospital
but only went

*

one night,

*

when you could have had the flu
but didn't;
when I could have climbed over those wailing bodies
at the funeral to sit by the bartender I spent

*

one night

with and weep beside him over the end of your life
and what I had done to him
and you;

It was wrong to leave you in that hospital room to suffer so
afraid to move across the pew so many seasons later I feel
like a book with a broken spine; fold like an umbrella tired
of fighting off rain I remember him now all the time now I

*

remember you.

CAKE

Wishing for slenderness, the fat man eats
an entire cake with his hands. Craving
freedom, the young girl takes a full-time job
with a boss who berates her. You wake up
and want the night back. You want to go back
to sleep. The man you love with the girlfriend
keeps asking if he can see you. You say
Yes and wonder why you tire easily
and are alone. You say you want nearness,
then move away from everyone you love.

NERVE

He said the pink cloud you feel
when you first come off alcohol
is not a pink cloud, it is
humility. The girl remembered
this in a cubicle on Monday,
three weeks after breaking up
with her boyfriend she saw
him online, his profile posted
on nerve.com. She remembered
the pink cloud she felt when they met
which she called love and her friend
Sarah John called "Not yet, but
maybe someday." How the cloud
scattered the Sunday she left New
York for Laguna Beach to work
for six months in front of a screen
where she clicked on a link
that opened his face. His height,
his weight, what he wanted.
She thought humility was seeing
her ex-boyfriend searching for
someone who was not her for play
or dating. She thought about him
Saturday night at the Crystal Palace
on Buck Owens Boulevard
in Bakersfield; how he would have
appreciated hearing Buck sing.
For once, she felt proud to be from
a place of which she had always been
ashamed. Night darkening on
the streets, sky trimmed in a veil
of hot pink clouds dragged
clear across the bleak horizon.

TRYING TO WRITE A SOUTHERN POEM

from a cubicle in downtown Manhattan
is not as easy as moving from Bakersfield,
California, to Syracuse, New York, to Chicago,
Illinois, *Il-a-noise,* my mother says, to the East
Village to SoHo, South of Houston, that is—
*How*ston in Manhattan, *Hue*ston
everywhere else, while you remain in Louisiana
between collard greens and the blues.

FLUSH

One night in New York on Thompson
between Spring and Prince you sat
down beside me in leather pants
sat down beside me on a wooden bench
under a street lamp, midnight sky,
moon so bright a man across the street
mistook it for the sun; under this moon
so luminescent you spoke of a woman
you once loved and love still,
spoke of what comes in the silence
of street lamps and boxes of photographs. *And this is where she used to
work.* This is where you circled the block
in search of her, studied light in her eyes
the night your bodies caught fire, this is
the same park same fence you climbed
after fighting until your face bled
tears of your heart beating between
your ribs like a bird trying to break
free, out of the iron gate of your body
out of a moon so bright you sat down
beside me on a wooden bench,
yesterday's sun asleep in your hair
woman you once loved and love still
alive in the jail of the past,
singing her song of what was/could be/
wasn't/isn't and may never come again,
you sat like a child sits over a toilet
unable to hold it any longer unable to help
looking into the water to see what you have

done, see what has passed through your body
has passed through us all and left
without asking if we were ready to go,
left so something green and good and whole
could enter again and leave the same way
like all things do and will and must
if we are able to stop asking yesterday's
remains to reenter us so we can be new again
we can begin again if we can look back,
let go and be courageous enough to flush.

WOODSTOCK

There is no such thing as going away.
There is a white house, a white fence
tucked in thick blankets of snow
in Woodstock. There are six of us
out of our starless city for days
that bleed into nights of olives
and eggplant, red sauce and wine
and wine and wine. And he drinks
and is happy. He looks at me while
I'm empty handed. *My God,* he says,
you do nothing. My eyes were like his
once like soft yellow flames dancing
in a fire. He wants to see me naked,
without my grandmother's ring.
Everyone goes away.
This is what I remember. He climbs
the stairs and says no goodnight.
I find him passed out in bed where he
lies still while I take off everything
and kiss his closed eyes. Look at me.
Look how much I've learned over
the endless winters; I know how to do this
all by myself, in the dark. How to cry
and not wake or move or touch
whatever body lands beside me;
how to slip off my grandmother's
jewelry but I don't know after all this
time how to prepare for her dying.
Two o'clock in the morning and I
can't sleep. Downstairs chunks of ice

sail down the frozen creek.
I want my grandmother back.
I want my mother's hands wrapped
around mine, want the California sun
to shine off all this ice and give me
the sunrise. Give me the morning
when light rips through the lace curtains
and I feel, finally, at home.

CALIFORNIA '97

At some stage of the workday I became
obsessed with wine. It was five o'clock,
slow. Sun blasted through the photo
studio windows. I had already ironed
the clothes for the models, undressed
and dressed them, zipped and tucked
them, tied their shoes. Now they were
on set, pretending to laugh, and I was
back in the wardrobe/closet, time passing
slow as traffic staggering toward the
Holland Tunnel. I was waiting for a party
to begin for the last company I quit over
an incident involving an Israeli man
who left me standing on a raining corner;
I was wondering what kind of wine
to bring my old boss and decided to ask
my new boss since he was French
and the French care about these kind
of questions. This is what time is like:
not knowing what to do but who
to ask for help. He said California
'97 was the best. I felt embarrassed,
being from California myself, not
knowing which seasons were rich
and which ones failed. I brought
the bottle to the party where the man
who decided not to like me last
summer decided he liked me now
that he was drunk, the spirit in
him lifted like steam from the sewer.

This is my life: a dance of age
and regret. Grapes picked and squashed
and who's to say which crops failed
and which turned to purple gold
in the dark cellar of the seasons. I am
kissing a man who sees three of me
before him. Who's to say which one
of me I am, or which state will be
the best after time has pressed itself
against it. For now I know the fruit
is ripe and all the wine's been spilled.

AGAINST ROMANCE

I am writing the romance out of the night
you pushed my hair out of my eyes while we stood
outside the seaside house owned by the rich guy from Texas
who couldn't stop drinking but let you sleep on his couch
for free. You said you were clean. Two nights later,
your breath on my spine, mouth on my neck, massive black
hair in my hands. A season later, I am editing the girlfriend
I helped you betray back into memory. *I am not that kind
of girl*, I kept saying, being that kind of girl. In the end,
you wanted romance from me. You wanted to leave
the woman you loved before she left you. Weeks later
your cologne continued to perfume my pillow. Sun kept setting,
trees kept taking their leaves off and trying on new ones,
and I kept falling asleep to the easy music of your voice
the night it began and ended, kissing and screaming
I can't I can't I cant . . .

SCREW

You have a girlfriend and I don't want to screw
another woman's man I said in the car overlooking
Catalina before I let him climb on top me so you can
imagine how that was hard to believe. Why
don't you go fuck Frank my last boyfriend screamed
when I told him I was moving to California. Then
he called crying from the street to apologize
moments after I threw him out. That was very Ike
Turner said the playright. This one pulls stolen
steak out of his pants, lights a cigarette and turns
the music up loud. I can't be with you I explain
running my hands over his mother's name
tattooed on his chest, his gang name on his stomach.
Four men park beside us on the cliff and get out
of their car to stare at the Pacific. He says I hope
they don't kiss. The mystic says What is spirit asking
you to do? Maybe we can get down/Maybe we can
get down, goes the song. Sarah says you may have to
screw him even though you know it's wrong and if you do,
take pictures and tell him your friend in Brooklyn
wants to see what he looks like. There is no right
or wrong, only pain. When he leaves, a ceaseless aching
that keeps me awake, studying blades on the ceiling
fan. Makes me drive to Macy's to buy three-inch black
stilletos on a Sunday. Eventually, I'll spin this
suffering into a kind of beauty. An afterglow,
luminous and full of heat. No moral compass,
no punishment for doing the so-called bad thing.
Some days I just want to listen to him breathe. Others,
his mouth in mine. Sure, the dotcom may tank

in a month and I'll return to New York and he'll be on
probation and unable leave the state. Does that mean
it won't work out? I don't love anyone, he says,
before you take me home you have to buy me
a burger. I say I can't be near you anymore.
This is the last kiss. He opens the door and walks
out of my life. When I said stop I meant Yes.
When I said leave I didn't realize he would do it.
Sarah says cheaters get cheated on but she had to
betray everyone she loved for years before she tried
something different. This afternoon her husband's
in the bedroom dressing their son Walter in striped
overalls and sneakers. I get tired of doing
the right thing the clouds get tired of holding back
all that rain until finally they surrender and drop
an ocean's worth of water on top of the car. Leave me
alone I say, enveloped in his arms.

WRITE ME A POEM

Write me a poem tonight,
I don't want to do this alone

Write it hard, while you bite my belly
Write it tight, while you hold me

Sing it long, and sing it deep
Make it sink into my flesh

Damp like the night tonight,
Write me a poem.

Tell me about German mothers,
Brothers with names like Nino

Dreams of calligraphy
Past lives in Korea

Tell me about growing up poor
On the South Side of Chicago—

Don't forget the taste of coffee
The morning after you needed her.

Read me poems you never write—
Talk to *me*

In words that make the alphabet dance
Talk to *me*

In sounds that make your heart beat fast.
Tell me you want to hold me

Like a drum between your thighs
And pound your rhythm in me

Find me in the fading light tonight
And write me a poem.

Compose it on recycled paper
Not pretending to be pure but white

Like my body smashed pulpy
Beneath stones of an angry father

Once a wild, living girl
Now just dry and tired

Write me again.
Turn me into a woman who is stronger

Taller, more vegetarian than I already am
Make me wise

And quiet, shy as a lamb
Paint it with blood, semen, the sweetness

Found only between a woman's legs—
Give me paintings and violins

Neatly tucked away in cedar chests
Make me alive tonight, a woman and

Broadcast lines you would never read aloud
Words only we would understand

Without judgment
Tell me I will never be a perfect ten,

That you'll settle for the eleven
I already am

Give me poems that turn your blue eyes green
With desire that's tender, ticklish as your skin

Sing me your secrets and shout them out loud
Blow them up secrets

Of brothers who disappeared
Unhappy mothers who were never near

Dying grandmothers for whom
No one cares

Sing me your fears
Buried deep in bones and misery

Buried black in Trinidad
Dance for me a poem

Sway like smoke between fingers
With chocolate ablaze in teeth of ivory

Speak stories, psalms you know by heart
From the book I never read because I don't believe

Give me
Something to believe in.

Give me a poem that brings you to tears
Takes you home like I never could

Make it quick,
Like you left me.

Make it under three minutes
Pleasing for you, *hell* on me

Draw boundaries thick and dark between us
Etch them backward on my forehead

And send me to a mirror because
I do not wish to see them

Carve lines that divide us since war, famine
Drugs and violence don't seem to—

Give me a poem that doesn't care about
Rambling revolutions, postmodern politics

Or poetic slam, but whispers in the quiet
In the soft of your lips touching mine

Give me a poem that makes me want to shave my legs
One that takes a chance

On a girl who can't be saved
Just this once—

Humor me, or hold me
Touch me with your winter weathered hands

And rock me, and love me
Leave me like you never can

And need me like you never will
Again

Write me a poem
I don't want to do this alone

NOTES

"Fahrenheit" is for Nancy Park.

"Différance" is for Felice Belle.

"Fall, New York," is in memory of
Captain Patrick Brown, Ladder 3.

"Hungry Charlie's" is in memory of
Fred Wolf.

ABOUT THE AUTHOR

Jennifer Murphy was born in Bakersfield, California, in 1975 and educated at Syracuse University and the University of Chicago. She lives in New York City.